Liturgy Documentary Series 8

Order of Christian Funerals

GENERAL INTRODUCTION AND PASTORAL NOTES

CONTENTS

Foreword.. 1

Decree of the Congregation for Divine Worship 5

Decree of the National Conference of Catholic Bishops 7

General Introduction 9

Ministry and Participation.. 10

Ministry for the Mourners and the Deceased 12

Liturgical Elements.. 14

Selection of the Rites from the Order of Christian Funerals..................... 19

Part I: Funeral Rites.. 21

Vigil and Related Rites and Prayers... 23

Vigil for the Deceased 24

Related Rites and Prayers 26

Prayers after Death... 27

Gathering in the Presence of the Body... 27

Transfer of the Body to the Church or to the Place of Committal..................... 28

Funeral Liturgy.. 29

Funeral Mass... 34

Funeral Liturgy outside Mass.. 35

Rite of Committal... 37

Part II: Funeral Rites for Children... 41

Vigil 43

Vigil for a Deceased Child.. 43

Funeral Liturgy.. 45

Funeral Mass... 46

Funeral Liturgy outside Mass.. 46

Rite of Committal... 49

Part III: Texts of Sacred Scripture 51

Part IV: Office for the Dead 53

Appendix I

Introduction to the 1969 *Ordo Exsequiarum* 61

   Offices and Ministries toward the Dead 64

   Adaptations Belonging to the Conference of Bishops 65

   Function of the Priest in Preparing and Planning the Celebration 66

Appendix II

Instruction on Cremation 71

Letter on Ecclesiastical Burial for Christians Involved in an Irregular Marriage .. 73

Decree on Ecclesiastical Burial 75

FOREWORD

In today's fast-paced world, one may get the impression that there are few things that are constant and can be depended upon. One constant, however, is that of birth; we have all been born into this changing world with its joys and sorrows. Equally certain is the reality of death; for as each of us has been born, inevitably each of us will face death.

For some persons death is annihilation; for others it is senseless and has no meaning. But for the Christian, death is a transition to a new and never-ending life. We believe that "life is changed, not ended." And "when the body of our earthly dwelling lies in death, we gain an everlasting dwelling place in heaven." This is all possible because in Christ, "who rose from the dead, our hope of resurrection has dawned. The sadness of death gives way to the bright promise of immortality."

One of the first rites to be revised after the Second Vatican Council was the *Rite of Funerals,* which was published in Latin in 1969 and in English in 1971. Now, eighteen years later, a revised English version of this rite has been published. The *Order of Christian Funerals* represents both a retranslation and an enrichment of the funeral rites for the English-speaking world. The International Commission on English in the Liturgy has provided us with a collection of rites intended for use from the time immediately after death until the body is committed to its final resting place.

One of the most important features of the *Order of Christian Funerals* is the inclusion of pastoral notes in each section of the book. These notes are intended to assist liturgical ministers and others who have responsibility for the pastoral care of mourners and for the preparation and celebration of the various rites connected with funerals. It is hoped that these pastoral notes and the general introduction of the *Order* will be read carefully by all who bear such responsibilities.

When God calls us, may we too "join the angels and saints as they sing their unending hymn of praise." For Christ has conquered sin and death and in him "darkness vanishes for ever."

Reverend Ronald F. Krisman
Executive Director
Secretariat for the Liturgy
National Conference of Catholic Bishops

1

THE ROMAN RITUAL

Revised by Decree of the Second Vatican Ecumenical Council
and Published by Authority of Pope Paul VI

ORDER OF
CHRISTIAN FUNERALS

The English translation of the "General Introduction," the "Pastoral Notes"
and the "Introduction to the 1969 *Ordo Exsequiarum*"
prepared by the
International Commission on English in the Liturgy,
a Joint Commission of Catholic Bishops' Conferences

CONGREGATION FOR DIVINE WORSHIP

Prot. no. 720/69

DECREE

By means of the funeral rites it has been the practice of the Church, as a tender mother, not simply to commend the dead to God but also to raise high the hope of its children and to give witness to its own faith in the future resurrection of the baptized with Christ.

Vatican Council II accordingly directed in the *Constitution on the Liturgy* that the funeral rites be revised in such a way that they would more clearly express the paschal character of the Christian's death and also that the rites for the burial of children would have a proper Mass (art. 81-82).

The Consilium prepared the desired rites and put them into trial use in different parts of the world. Now Pope Paul VI by his apostolic authority has approved and ordered the publication of these rites as henceforth obligatory for all those using the Roman Ritual.

Also by order of Pope Paul this Congregation for Divine Worship promulgates the *Order of Funerals,* stipulating that its effective date is 1 June 1970.

The Congregation further establishes that until 1 June 1970 when Latin is used in celebrating funerals there is an option to use either the present rite or the rite now in the Roman Ritual; after 1 June 1970 only this new *Order of Funerals* is to be used.

Once the individual conferences of bishops have prepared a vernacular version of the rite and received its confirmation from this Congregation, they have authorization to fix any other, feasible effective date prior to 1 June 1970 for use of the *Order of Funerals.*

5

All things to the contrary notwithstanding.

Congregation for Divine Worship, 15 August 1969, the solemnity of the Assumption.

+Benno Cardinal Gut
Prefect

Annibale Bugnini
Secretary

NATIONAL CONFERENCE OF CATHOLIC BISHOPS UNITED STATES OF AMERICA

DECREE

In accord with the norms established by decree of the Sacred Congregation of Rites *Cum, nostra aetate* (27 January 1966), the *Order of Christian Funerals* is declared to be the vernacular typical edition of the *Ordo Exesequiarum* for the dioceses of the United States of America and may be published by authority of the National Conference of Catholic Bishops.

The *Order of Christian Funerals* was canonically approved by the National Conference of Catholic Bishops in plenary assembly on 14 November 1985 and was subsequently confirmed by the Apostolic See by decree of the Congregation for Divine Worship on 29 April 1987 (Prot. N. CD 1550/85).

On 1 October 1989 the *Order of Christian Funerals* may be published and used in funeral celebrations. From All Souls Day, 2 November 1989, its use is mandatory in the dioceses of the United States of America. From that date forward no other English version of these rites may be used.

Given at the General Secretariat of the National Conference of Catholic Bishops, Washington, D.C., on 15 August 1989, the Solemnity of the Assumption.

+John L. May
Archbishop of Saint Louis
President
National Conference of Catholic Bishops

Robert N. Lynch
General Secretary

7

GENERAL INTRODUCTION

1   In the face of death, the Church confidently proclaims that God has created each person for eternal life and that Jesus, the Son of God, by his death and resurrection, has broken the chains of sin and death that bound humanity. Christ "achieved his task of redeeming humanity and giving perfect glory to God, principally by the paschal mystery of his blessed passion, resurrection from the dead, and glorious ascension."[1]

2   The proclamation of Jesus Christ "who was put to death for our sins and raised to life to justify us" (Romans 4:25) is at the center of the Church's life. The mystery of the Lord's death and resurrection gives power to all of the Church's activity. "For it was from the side of Christ as he slept the sleep of death upon the cross that there came forth the sublime sacrament of the whole Church."[2] The Church's liturgical and sacramental life and proclamation of the Gospel make this mystery present in the life of the faithful. Through the sacraments of baptism, confirmation, and eucharist, men and women are initiated into this mystery. "You have been taught that when we were baptized in Christ Jesus we were baptized into his death; in other words when we were baptized we went into the tomb with him and joined him in death, so that as Christ was raised from the dead by the Father's glory, we too might live a new life. If in union with Christ we have imitated his death, we shall also imitate him in his resurrection" (Romans 6:3-5).

3   In the eucharistic sacrifice, the Church's celebration of Christ's Passover from death to life, the faith of the baptized in the paschal mystery is renewed and nourished. Their union with Christ and with each other is strengthened: "Because there is one bread, we who are many, are one body, for we all partake of the one bread" (1 Corinthians 10:17).

4   At the death of a Christian, whose life of faith was begun in the waters of baptism and strengthened at the eucharistic table, the Church intercedes on behalf of the deceased because of its confident belief that death is not the end nor does it break the bonds forged in life. The Church also ministers to the

---

[1] Vatican Council II, Constitution on the Liturgy *Sacrosanctum Concilium,* art. 5.

[2] Ibid.

sorrowing and consoles them in the funeral rites with the comforting word of God and the sacrament of the eucharist.

5   Christians celebrate the funeral rites to offer worship, praise, and thanksgiving to God for the gift of a life which has now been returned to God, the author of life and the hope of the just. The Mass, the memorial of Christ's death and resurrection, is the principal celebration of the Christian funeral.

6   The Church through its funeral rites commends the dead to God's merciful love and pleads for the forgiveness of their sins. At the funeral rites, especially at the celebration of the eucharistic sacrifice, the Christian community affirms and expresses the union of the Church on earth with the Church in heaven in the one great communion of saints. Though separated from the living, the dead are still at one with the community of believers on earth and benefit from their prayers and intercession. At the rite of final commendation and farewell, the community acknowledges the reality of separation and commends the deceased to God. In this way it recognizes the spiritual bond that still exists between the living and the dead and proclaims its belief that all the faithful will be raised up and reunited in the new heavens and a new earth, where death will be no more.

7   The celebration of the Christian funeral brings hope and consolation to the living. While proclaiming the Gospel of Jesus Christ and witnessing to Christian hope in the resurrection, the funeral rites also recall to all who take part in them God's mercy and judgment and meet the human need to turn always to God in times of crisis.

MINISTRY AND PARTICIPATION

8   "If one member suffers in the body of Christ which is the Church, all the members suffer with that member" (1 Corinthians 12:26). For this reason, those who are baptized into Christ and nourished at the same table of the Lord are responsible for one another. When Christians are sick, their brothers and sisters share a ministry of mutual charity and "do all that they can to help the sick return to health, by showing love for the sick, and by celebrating the sacraments with them."[3] So too when a member of Christ's Body dies, the faithful are called to a ministry of consolation to those who have suffered the loss of one whom they love. Christian consolation is rooted in that hope that comes from faith in the saving death and resurrection of the Lord Jesus Christ. Christian hope faces the reality of death and the anguish of grief but trusts confidently that the power of sin and death has been vanquished by the risen Lord. The Church calls each member of Christ's Body—priest, deacon,

---

[3]   See Roman Ritual, *Pastoral Care of the Sick: Rites of Anointing and Viaticum*, General Introduction, no. 33.

layperson— to participate in the ministry of consolation: to care for the dying, to pray for the dead, to comfort those who mourn.

COMMUNITY

9   The responsibility for the ministry of consolation rests with the believing community, which heeds the words and example of the Lord Jesus: "Blessed are they who mourn; they shall be consoled" (Matthew 5:3). Each Christian shares in this ministry according to the various gifts and offices in the Church. As part of the pastoral ministry, pastors and associate pastors and other ministers should instruct the parish community on the Christian meaning of death and on the purpose and significance of the Church's liturgical rites for the dead. Information on how the parish community assists families in preparing for funerals should also be provided.

By giving instruction, pastors and associate pastors should lead the community to a deeper appreciation of its role in the ministry of consolation and to a fuller understanding of the significance of the death of a fellow Christian. Often the community must respond to the anguish voiced by Martha, the sister of Lazarus: "Lord, if you had been here, my brother would never have died" (John 11:21) and must console those who mourn, as Jesus himself consoled Martha: "Your brother will rise again. ... I am the resurrection and the life: those who believe in me, though they should die, will come to life; and those who are alive and believe in me will never die" (John 11:25-26). The faith of the Christian community in the resurrection of the dead brings support and strength to those who suffer the loss of those whom they love.

10   Members of the community should console the mourners with words of faith and support and with acts of kindness, for example, assisting them with some of the routine tasks of daily living. Such assistance may allow members of the family to devote time to planning the funeral rites with the priest and other ministers and may also give the family time for prayer and mutual comfort.

11   The community's principal involvement in the ministry of consolation is expressed in its active participation in the celebration of the funeral rites, particularly the vigil for the deceased, the funeral liturgy, and the rite of committal. For this reason these rites should be scheduled at times that permit as many of the community as possible to be present. The assembly's participation can be assisted by the preparation of booklets that contain an outline of the rite, the texts and songs belonging to the people, and directions for posture, gesture, and movement.

12   At the vigil for the deceased or on another occasion before the eucharistic celebration, the presiding minister should invite all to be present at the funeral liturgy and to take an active part in it. The minister may also describe the funeral liturgy and explain why the community gathers to hear the word of God proclaimed and to celebrate the eucharist when one of the faithful dies.

Pastors, associate pastors, and other ministers should also be mindful of those persons who are not members of the Catholic Church, or Catholics who are not involved in the life of the Church.

13 As a minister of reconciliation, the priest should be especially sensitive to the possible needs for reconciliation felt by the family and others. Funerals can begin the process of reconciling differences and supporting those ties that can help the bereaved adjust to the loss brought about by death. With attentiveness to each situation, the priest can help to begin the process of reconciliation when needed. In some cases this process may find expression in the celebration of the sacrament of penance, either before the funeral liturgy or at a later time.

LITURGICAL MINISTERS

Presiding Minister

14 Priests, as teachers of faith and ministers of comfort, preside at the funeral rites, especially the Mass; the celebration of the funeral liturgy is especially entrusted to pastors and associate pastors. When no priest is available, deacons, as ministers of the word, of the altar, and of charity, preside at funeral rites. When no priest or deacon is available for the vigil and related rites or the rite of committal, a layperson presides.

Other Liturgical Ministers

15 In the celebration of the funeral rites laymen and laywomen may serve as readers, musicians, ushers, pallbearers, and, according to existing norms, as special ministers of the eucharist. Pastors and other priests should instill in these ministers an appreciation of how much the reverent exercise of their ministries contributes to the celebration of the funeral rites. Family members should be encouraged to take an active part in these ministries, but they should not be asked to assume any role that their grief or sense of loss may make too burdensome.

MINISTRY FOR THE MOURNERS AND THE DECEASED

FAMILY AND FRIENDS

16 In planning and carrying out the funeral rites the pastor and all other ministers should keep in mind the life of the deceased and the circumstances

of death. They should also take into consideration the spiritual and psychological needs of the family and friends of the deceased to express grief and their sense of loss, to accept the reality of death, and to comfort one another.

17 Whenever possible, ministers should involve the family in planning the funeral rites: in the choice of texts and rites provided in the ritual, in the selection of music for the rites, and in the designation of liturgical ministers.

Planning of the funeral rites may take place during the visit of the pastor or other minister at some appropriate time after the death and before the vigil service. Ministers should explain to the family the meaning and significance of each of the funeral rites, especially the vigil, the funeral liturgy, and the rite of committal.

If pastoral and personal considerations allow, the period before death may be an appropriate time to plan the funeral rites with the family and even with the family member who is dying. Although planning the funeral before death should be approached with sensitivity and care, it can have the effect of helping the one who is dying and the family face the reality of death with Christian hope. It can also help relieve the family of numerous details after the death and may allow them to benefit more fully from the celebration of the funeral rites.

DECEASED

18 Through the celebration of the funeral rites, the Church manifests its care for the dead, both baptized members and catechumens. In keeping with the provisions of *Codex Iuris Canonici,* can. 1183, the Church's funeral rites may be celebrated for a child who died before baptism and whose parents intended to have the child baptized.

At the discretion of the local Ordinary, the Church's funeral rites may be celebrated for a baptized member of another Church or ecclesial community provided this would not be contrary to the wishes of the deceased person and provided the minister of the Church or ecclesial community in which the deceased person was a regular member or communicant is unavailable.

19 Since in baptism the body was marked with the seal of the Trinity and became the temple of the Holy Spirit, Christians respect and honor the bodies of the dead and the places where they rest. Any customs associated with the preparation of the body of the deceased should always be marked with dignity and reverence and never with the despair of those who have no hope. Preparation of the body should include prayer, especially at those intimate moments reserved for family members. For the final disposition of the body, it is the ancient Christian custom to bury or entomb the bodies of the dead; cremation is permitted, unless it is evident that cremation was chosen for anti-Christian motives.

20 In countries or regions where an undertaker, and not the family or community, carries out the preparation and transfer of the body, the pastor

and other ministers are to ensure that the undertakers appreciate the values and beliefs of the Christian community.

The family and friends of the deceased should not be excluded from taking part in the services sometimes provided by undertakers, for example, the preparation and laying out of the body.

LITURGICAL ELEMENTS

21   Since liturgical celebration involves the whole person, it requires attentiveness to all that affects the senses. The readings and prayers, psalms and songs should be proclaimed or sung with understanding, conviction, and reverence. Music for the assembly should be truly expressive of the texts and at the same time simple and easily sung. The ritual gestures, processions, and postures should express and foster an attitude of reverence and reflectiveness in those taking part in the funeral rites. The funeral rites should be celebrated in an atmosphere of simple beauty, in a setting that encourages participation. Liturgical signs and symbols affirming Christian belief and hope in the paschal mystery are abundant in the celebration of the funeral rites, but their undue multiplication or repetition should be avoided. Care must be taken that the choice and use of signs and symbols are in accord with the culture of the people.

THE WORD OF GOD

Readings

22   In every celebration for the dead, the Church attaches great importance to the reading of the word of God. The readings proclaim to the assembly the paschal mystery, teach remembrance of the dead, convey the hope of being gathered together again in God's kingdom, and encourage the witness of Christian life. Above all, the readings tell of God's designs for a world in which suffering and death will relinquish their hold on all whom God has called his own. A careful selection and use of readings from Scripture for the funeral rites will provide the family and the community with an opportunity to hear God speak to them in their needs, sorrows, fears, and hopes.

23   In the celebration of the liturgy of the word at the funeral liturgy, the biblical readings may not be replaced by nonbiblical readings. But during prayer services with the family nonbiblical readings may be used in addition to readings from Scripture.

24   Liturgical tradition assigns the proclamation of the readings in the celebration of the liturgy of the word to readers and the deacon. The presiding minister proclaims the readings only when there are no assisting ministers present. Those designated to proclaim the word of God should prepare themselves to exercise this ministry.[4]

Psalmody

25   The psalms are rich in imagery, feeling, and symbolism. They powerfully express the suffering and pain, the hope and trust of people of every age and culture. Above all the psalms sing of faith in God, of revelation and redemption. They enable the assembly to pray in the words that Jesus himself used during his life on earth. Jesus, who knew anguish and the fear of death, "offered up prayer and entreaty, aloud and in silent tears, to the one who had the power to save him out of death. . . . Although he was Son, he learned to obey through suffering; but having been made perfect, he became for all who obey him the source of eternal salvation . . ." (Hebrews 5:7-9). In the psalms the members of the assembly pray in the voice of Christ, who intercedes on their behalf before the Father.[5] The Church, like Christ, turns again and again to the psalms as a genuine expression of grief and of praise and as a sure source of trust and hope in times of trial. Pastors and other ministers are, therefore, to make an earnest effort through an effective catechesis to lead their communities to a clearer and deeper grasp of at least some of the psalms provided for the funeral rites.

26   The psalms are designated for use in many places in the funeral rites (for example, as responses to the readings, for the processions, for use at the vigil for the deceased). Since the psalms are songs, whenever possible, they should be sung.

Homily

27   A brief homily based on the readings is always given after the gospel reading at the funeral liturgy and may also be given after the readings at the vigil service; but there is never to be a eulogy. Attentive to the grief of those present, the homilist should dwell on God's compassionate love and on the paschal mystery of the Lord, as proclaimed in the Scripture readings. The homilist should also help the members of the assembly to understand that the mystery of God's love and the mystery of Jesus' victorious death and resurrection were present in the life and death of the deceased and that these mysteries are active in their own lives as well. Through the homily members of the family and community should receive consolation and strength to face

---

[4]   See Lectionary for Mass (2nd *editio typica*, 1981), General Introduction, nos. 49, 52, and 55.
[5]   See General Instruction of the Liturgy of the Hours, no. 109.

the death of one of their members with a hope nourished by the saving word of God. Laypersons who preside at the funeral rites give an instruction on the readings.

PRAYERS AND INTERCESSIONS

28 In the presidential prayers of the funeral rites the presiding minister addresses God on behalf of the deceased and the mourners in the name of the entire Church. From the variety of prayers provided the minister in consultation with the family should carefully select texts that truly capture the unspoken prayers and hopes of the assembly and also respond to the needs of the mourners.

29 Having heard the word of God proclaimed and preached, the assembly responds at the vigil and at the funeral liturgy with prayers of intercession for the deceased and all the dead, for the family and all who mourn, and for all in the assembly. The holy people of God, confident in their belief in the communion of saints, exercise their royal priesthood by joining together in this prayer for all those who have died.[6]

Several models of intercessions are provided within the rites for adaptation to the circumstances.

MUSIC

30 Music is integral to the funeral rites. It allows the community to express convictions and feelings that words alone may fail to convey. It has the power to console and uplift the mourners and to strengthen the unity of the assembly in faith and love. The texts of the songs chosen for a particular celebration should express the paschal mystery of the Lord's suffering, death, and triumph over death and should be related to the readings from Scripture.

31 Since music can evoke strong feelings, the music for the celebration of the funeral rites should be chosen with great care. The music at funerals should support, console, and uplift the participants and should help to create in them a spirit of hope in Christ's victory over death and in the Christian's share in that victory.

32 Music should be provided for the vigil and funeral liturgy and, whenever possible, for the funeral processions and the rite of committal. The specific notes that precede each of these rites suggest places in the rites where music is appropriate. Many musical settings used by the parish community during the liturgical year may be suitable for use at funerals. Efforts should be made to develop and expand the parish's repertoire for use at funerals.

---

[6] See *De Oratione communi seu fidelium* (2nd ed., Vatican Polyglot Press, 1966), chapter 1, no. 3, p. 7: tr., *Documents on the Liturgy* (The Liturgical Press, 1982), no. 1893.

33   An organist or other instrumentalist, a cantor, and, whenever possible, even a choir should assist the assembly's full participation in singing the songs, responses, and acclamations of these rites.

SILENCE

34   Prayerful silence is an element important to the celebration of the funeral rites. Intervals of silence should be observed, for example, after each reading and during the final commendation and farewell, to permit the assembly to reflect upon the word of God and the meaning of the celebration.

SYMBOLS

Easter Candle and Other Candles

35   The Easter candle reminds the faithful of Christ's undying presence among them, of his victory over sin and death, and of their share in that victory by virtue of their initiation. It recalls the Easter Vigil, the night when the Church awaits the Lord's resurrection and when new light for the living and the dead is kindled. During the funeral liturgy and also during the vigil service, when celebrated in the church, the Easter candle may be placed beforehand near the position the coffin will occupy at the conclusion of the procession.

According to local custom, other candles may also be placed near the coffin during the funeral liturgy as a sign of reverence and solemnity.

Holy Water

36   Blessed or holy water reminds the assembly of the saving waters of baptism. In the rite of reception of the body at the church, its use calls to mind the deceased's baptism and initiation into the community of faith. In the rite of final commendation the gesture of sprinkling may also signify farewell.

Incense

37   Incense is used during the funeral rites as a sign of honor to the body of the deceased, which through baptism became the temple of the Holy Spirit. Incense is also used as a sign of the community's prayers for the deceased rising to the throne of God and as a sign of farewell.

Other Symbols

38   If it is the custom in the local community, a pall may be placed over the coffin when it is received at the church. A reminder of the baptismal garment of the deceased, the pall is a sign of the Christian dignity of the person. The use of the pall also signifies that all are equal in the eyes of God (see James 2:1-9).

A Book of the Gospels or a Bible may be placed on the coffin as a sign that Christians live by the word of God and that fidelity to that word leads to eternal life.

A cross may be placed on the coffin as a reminder that the Christian is marked by the cross in baptism and through Jesus' suffering on the cross is brought to the victory of his resurrection.

Fresh flowers, used in moderation, can enhance the setting of the funeral rites.

Only Christian symbols may rest on or be placed near the coffin during the funeral liturgy. Any other symbols, for example, national flags, or flags or insignia of associations, have no place in the funeral liturgy (cf. no. 132).

Liturgical Color

39   The liturgical color chosen for funerals should express Christian hope but should not be offensive to human grief or sorrow. In the United States, white, violet, or black vestments may be worn at the funeral rites and at other offices and Masses for the dead.

RITUAL GESTURES AND MOVEMENT

40   The presiding minister or an assisting minister may quitely direct the assembly in the movements, gestures, and posture appropriate to the particular ritual moment or action.

41   Processions, especially when accompanied with music and singing, can strengthen the bond of communion in the assembly. For processions, ministers of music should give preference to settings of psalms and songs that are responsorial or litanic in style and that allow the people to respond to the verses with an invariable refrain. During the various processions, it is preferable that the pallbearers carry the coffin as a sign of reverence and respect for the deceased.

42   Processions continue to have special significance in funeral celebrations, as in Christian Rome where funeral rites consisted of three "stages" or "stations" joined by two processions. Christians accompanied the body on its last journey. From the home of the deceased the Christian community proceeded to the church singing psalms. When the service in the church concluded, the

body was carried in solemn procession to the grave or tomb. During the final procession the congregation sang psalms praising the God of mercy and redemption and antiphons entrusting the deceased to the care of the angels and saints. The funeral liturgy mirrored the journey of human life, the Christian pilgrimage to the heavenly Jerusalem.

In many places and situations a solemn procession on foot to the church or to the place of committal may not be possible. Nevertheless at the conclusion of the funeral liturgy an antiphon or versicle and response may be sung as the body is taken to the entrance of the church. Psalms, hymns, or liturgical songs may also be sung when the participants gather at the place of committal.

SELECTION OF RITES FROM
THE ORDER OF CHRISTIAN FUNERALS

43   The *Order of Christian Funerals* makes provision for the minister, in consultation with the family, to choose those rites and texts that are most suitable to the situation: those that most closely apply to the needs of the mourners, the circumstances of the death, and the customs of the local Christian community. The minister and family may be assisted in the choice of a rite or rites by the reflections preceding each rite or group of rites.

44   Part I, "Funeral Rites," of the *Order of Christian Funerals* provides those rites that may be used in the funerals of Christians and is divided into three groups of rites that correspond in general to the three principal ritual moments in Christian funerals: "Vigil and Related Rites and Prayers," "Funeral Liturgy," and "Rite of Committal."

45   The section entitled "Vigil and Related Rites and Prayers" includes rites that may be celebrated between the time of death and the funeral liturgy or, should there be no funeral liturgy, before the rite of committal. The vigil is the principal celebration of the Christian community during the time before the funeral liturgy. It may take the form of a liturgy of the word (see nos. 54-97) or of some part of the office for the dead (see Part IV, nos. 348-395). Two vigil services are provided: "Vigil for the Deceased" and "Vigil for the Deceased with Reception at the Church." The second service is used when the vigil is celebrated in the church and the body is to be received at this time.

"Related Rites and Prayers" includes three brief rites that may be used on occasions of prayer with the family: "Prayers after Death," "Gathering in the Presence of the Body," and "Transfer of the Body to the Church or to the Place of Committal." These rites are examples or models of what can be done and should be adapted to the circumstances.

46   The section entitled "Funeral Liturgy" provides two forms of the funeral liturgy, the central celebration of the Christian community for the deceased:

"Funeral Mass" and "Funeral Liturgy outside Mass." When one of its members dies, the Church especially encourages the celebration of the Mass. When Mass cannot be celebrated (see no. 178), the second form of the funeral liturgy may be used and a Mass for the deceased should be celebrated, if possible, at a later time.

47   The section entitled "Rite of Committal" includes two forms of the rite of committal, the concluding rite of the funeral: "Rite of Committal" and "Rite of Committal with Final Commendation." The first form is used when the final commendation is celebrated as part of the conclusion of the funeral liturgy. The second form is used when the final commendation does not take place during the funeral liturgy or when no funeral liturgy precedes the committal.

48   Part II, "Funeral Rites for Children," provides an adaptation of the principal rites in Part I: "Vigil for a Deceased Child," Funeral Liturgy," and "Rite of Committal." These rites may be used in the funerals of infants and young children, including those of early school age. The rites in Part II include texts for use in the case of a baptized child and in the case of a child who died before baptism.

In some instances, for example, the death of an infant, the vigil and funeral liturgy may not be appropriate. Only the rite of committal and perhaps one of the forms of prayer with the family as provided in "Related Rites and Prayers" may be desirable. Part II does not contain "Related Rites and Prayers," but the rites from Part I may be adapted.

49   Part III, "Texts from Sacred Scripture," includes the Scripture readings and psalms for the celebration of the funeral rites. Part IV, "Office for the Dead," includes "Morning Prayer," "Evening Prayer," and "Additional Hymns." Part V, "Additional Texts," contains "Prayers and Texts in Particular Circumstances" and "Holy Communion outside Mass." The texts that appear in the various rites in Parts I, II, and IV may be replaced by corresponding readings and psalms given in Part III and by corresponding prayers and texts given in Part V.

PART I
FUNERAL RITES

God is not the God of the dead but of the living;
for in him all are alive

50   Part I of the *Order of Christian Funerals* is divided into three groups of
rites that correspond in general to the three principal ritual moments in the
funerals of Christians: "Vigil and Related Rites and Prayers," "Funeral Liturgy,"
and "Rite of Committal." The minister, in consultation with those concerned,
chooses from within these three groups of rites those that best correspond to
the particular needs and customs of the mourners. This choice may be assisted
by the reflections given in the General Introduction and in the introduction
to each rite or group of rites.

VIGIL AND RELATED RITES
AND PRAYERS

Do not let your hearts be troubled; trust in God still

51   The rites provided here may be celebrated between the time of death and the funeral liturgy or, should there be no funeral liturgy, before the rite of committal. Two forms of the vigil are presented here: "Vigil for the Deceased," and "Vigil for the Deceased with Reception at the Church," for convenient use in accord with the circumstances.

"Related Rites and Prayers" includes three brief rites that may be used on occasions of prayer with the family: "Prayers after Death," "Gathering in the Presence of the Body," and "Transfer of the Body to the Church or to the Place of Committal." These rites are examples or models of what can be done and should be adapted to the circumstances.

52   The time immediately following death is often one of bewilderment and may involve shock or heartrending grief for the family and close friends. The ministry of the Church at this time is one of gently accompanying the mourners in their initial adjustment to the fact of death and to the sorrow this entails. Through a careful use of the rites contained in this section, the minister helps the mourners to express their sorrow and to find strength and consolation through faith in Christ and his resurrection to eternal life. The members of the Christian community offer support to the mourners, especially by praying that the one they have lost may have eternal life.

53   Ministers should be aware that the experience of death can bring about in the mourners possible needs for reconciliation. With attentiveness to each situation, the minister can help to begin the process of reconciliation. In some cases this process may find expression in the celebration of the sacrament of penance, either before the funeral liturgy or at a later time.

VIGIL FOR THE DECEASED

Happy now are the dead who die in the Lord;
they shall find rest from their labors

54   The vigil for the deceased is the principal rite celebrated by the Christian community in the time following death and before the funeral liturgy, or if there is no funeral liturgy, before the rite of committal. It may take the form either of a liturgy of the word (nos. 69-81, 82-97) or of some part of the office for the dead (see Part IV, nos. 348-395). Two vigil services are provided: "Vigil for the Deceased" and "Vigil for the Deceased with Reception at the Church." The second service is used when the vigil is celebrated in the church and begins with the reception of the body.

55   The vigil may be celebrated in the home of the deceased, in the funeral home, parlor or chapel of rest, or in some other suitable place. It may also be celebrated in the church, but at a time well before the funeral liturgy, so that the funeral liturgy will not be lengthy and the liturgy of the word repetitious. Adaptations of the vigil will often be suggested by the place in which the celebration occurs. A celebration in the home of the deceased, for example, may be simplified and shortened.

    If the reception of the body at church is celebrated apart from the vigil or the funeral liturgy, the "Vigil for the Deceased with Reception at the Church" may be used and simplified.

56   At the vigil the Christian community keeps watch with the family in prayer to the God of mercy and finds strength in Christ's presence. It is the first occasion among the funeral rites for the solemn reading of the word of God. In this time of loss the family and community turn to God's word as the source of faith and hope, as light and life in the face of darkness and death. Consoled by the redeeming word of God and by the abiding presence of Christ and his Spirit, the assembly at the vigil calls upon the Father of mercy to receive the deceased into the kingdom of light and peace.

STRUCTURE

57   The vigil in the form of the liturgy of the word consists of the introductory rites, the liturgy of the word, the prayer of intercession, and a concluding rite.

Introductory Rites

58   The introductory rites gather the faithful together to form a community and to prepare all to listen to God's word. The introductory rites of the vigil

for the deceased include the greeting, an opening song, an invitation to prayer, a pause for silent prayer, and an opening prayer.

In the vigil for the deceased with reception at the church, the rite of reception forms the introductory rites (nos. 82-86). In this case the family and others who have accompanied the body are greeted at the entrance of the church. The body is then sprinkled with holy water and, if it is the custom, the pall is placed on the coffin by family members, friends, or the minister. The entrance procession follows, during which a hymn or psalm is sung. At the conclusion of the procession a symbol of the Christian life may be placed on the coffin. Then the invitation to prayer, a pause for silent prayer, and an opening prayer conclude the introductory rites.

The opening song or entrance song should be a profound expression of belief in eternal life and the resurrection of the dead, as well as a prayer of intercession for the dead.

Liturgy of the Word

59   The proclamation of the word of God is the high point and central focus of the vigil. The liturgy of the word usually includes a first reading, responsorial psalm, gospel reading, and homily. A reader proclaims the first reading. The responsorial psalm should be sung, whenever possible. If an assisting deacon is present, he proclaims the gospel reading. Otherwise the presiding minister proclaims the gospel reading.

60   The purpose of the readings at the vigil is to proclaim the paschal mystery, teach remembrance of the dead, convey the hope of being gathered together in God's kingdom, and encourage the witness of Christian life. Above all, the readings tell of God's designs for a world in which suffering and death will relinquish their hold on all whom God has called his own. The responsorial psalm enables the community to respond in faith to the reading and to express its grief and its praise of God. In the selection of readings the needs of the mourners and the circumstances of the death should be kept in mind.

61   A homily based on the readings is given at the vigil to help those present find strength and hope in God's saving word.

Prayer of Intercession

62   In the prayer of intercession the community calls upon God to comfort the mourners and to show mercy to the deceased. The prayer of intercession takes the form of a litany, the Lord's Prayer, and a concluding prayer.

After this prayer and before the blessing or at some other suitable time during the vigil, a member of the family or a friend of the deceased may speak in remembrance of the deceased.

Concluding Rite

63   The vigil concludes with a blessing, which may be followed by a liturgical song or a few moments of silent prayer or both.

MINISTRY AND PARTICIPATION

64   Members of the local parish community should be encouraged to participate in the vigil as a sign of concern and support for the mourners. In many circumstances the vigil will be the first opportunity for friends, neighbors, and members of the local parish community to show their concern for the family of the deceased by gathering for prayer. The vigil may also serve as an opportunity for participation in the funeral by those who, because of work or other reasons, cannot be present for the funeral liturgy or the rite of committal.
65   The full participation by all present is to be encouraged. This is best achieved through careful planning of the celebration. Whenever possible, the family of the deceased should take part in the selection of texts and music and in the designation of liturgical ministers.
66   Besides the presiding minister, other available ministers (a reader, a cantor, an acolyte) should exercise their ministries. Family members may assume some of these liturgical roles, unless their grief prevents them from doing so.

The presiding minister and assisting ministers should vest for the vigil according to local custom. If the vigil is celebrated in the church, a priest or deacon who presides wears an alb or surplice with stole.
67   As needs require, and especially if the funeral liturgy or rite of committal is not to take place for a few days, the vigil may be celebrated more than once and should be adapted to each occasion.
68   Music is integral to any vigil, especially the vigil for the deceased. In the difficult circumstances following death, well-chosen music can touch the mourners and others present at levels of human need that words alone often fail to reach. Such music can enliven the faith of the community gathered to support the family and to affirm hope in the resurrection.

Whenever possible, an instrumentalist and a cantor or leader of song should assist the assembly's full participation in the singing.

In the choice of music for the vigil, preference should be given to the singing of the opening song and the responsorial psalm. The litany, the Lord's Prayer, and a closing song may also be sung.

RELATED RITES AND PRAYERS

If we have died with Christ, we believe we shall also live with him

98   The section entitled "Related Rites and Prayers" contains three brief rites, "Prayers after Death," "Gathering in the Presence of the Body," and "Transfer

of the Body to the Church or to the Place of Committal." These rites are presented to help the minister and others pray with the family and close friends in the period soon after death. "Prayers after Death" may be used when the minister first meets with the family, "Gathering in the Presence of the Body," when the family first gathers together around the body of the deceased, and "Transfer of the Body to the Church or to the Place of Committal," when the family and friends prepare to accompany the body of the deceased in the procession to the church or to the place of committal.

99   These rites are signs of the concern of the Christian community for the family and close friends of the deceased. The compassionate presence of the minister and others and the familiar elements of these simple rites can have the effect of reassuring the mourners and of providing a consoling and hopeful situation in which to pray and to express the grief.

100 The circumstances for the celebration of these rites may vary from place to place and from culture to culture. The rites as given are only models, for adaptation by the minister according to the circumstances.

PRAYERS AFTER DEATH

Blessed are the sorrowing; they shall be consoled

101 This rite provides a model of prayer that may be used when the minister first meets with the family following death. The rite follows a common pattern of reading, response, prayer, and blessing and may be adapted according to the circumstances.

102 The presence of the minister and the calming effect of familiar prayers can comfort the mourners as they begin to face their loss. When the minister is present with the family at the time death occurs, this rite can be used as a quiet and prayerful response to the death. In other circumstances, for example, in the case of sudden or unexpected death, this form of prayer can be the principal part of the first pastoral visit of the minister.

103 The initial pastoral visit can be important as the first tangible expression of the community's support for the mourners. A minister unfamiliar with the family or the deceased person can learn a great deal on this occasion about the needs of the family and about the life of the deceased. The minister may also be able to form some preliminary judgments to help the family in planning the funeral rites. If circumstances allow, some first steps in the planning may take place at this time.

GATHERING IN THE PRESENCE OF THE BODY

If we have died with Christ, we believe we shall also live with him.

109 This rite provides a model of prayer that may be used when the family first gathers in the presence of the body, when the body is to be prepared for

burial, or after it has been prepared. The family members, in assembling in the presence of the body, confront in the most immediate way the fact of their loss and the mystery of death. Because cultural attitudes and practices on such occasions may vary, the minister should adapt the rite.

110 Through the presence of the minister and others and through the celebration of this brief rite, the community seeks to be with the mourners in their need and to provide an atmosphere of sensitive concern and confident faith. In prayer and gesture those present show reverence for the body of the deceased as a temple of the life-giving Spirit and ask, in that same Spirit, for the eternal life promised to the faithful.

111 The minister should try to be as attentive as possible to the particular needs of the mourners. The minister begins the rite at an opportune moment and, as much as possible, in an atmosphere of calm and recollection. The pause for silent prayer after the Scripture verse can be especially helpful in this regard.

TRANSFER OF THE BODY TO THE CHURCH OR TO THE PLACE OF COMMITTAL

Your life is hidden now with Christ in God

119 This rite may be used for prayer with the family and close friends as they prepare to accompany the body of the deceased in the procession to the church or to the place of committal. It is a model, for adaptation by the minister according to the circumstances.

120 The procession to the church is a rite of initial separation of the mourners from the deceased; the procession to the place of committal is the journey to the place of final separation of the mourners from the deceased. Because the transfer of the body may be an occasion of great emotion for the mourners, the minister and other members of the community should make every effort to be present to support them. Reverent celebration of the rite can help reassure the mourners and create an atmosphere of calm preparation before the procession.

FUNERAL LITURGY

All will be brought to life in Christ

128 The funeral liturgy is the central liturgical celebration of the Christian community for the deceased. Two forms of the funeral liturgy are presented here: "Funeral Mass" and "Funeral Liturgy outside Mass."

When one of its members dies, the Church encourages the celebration of the Mass. But when Mass cannot be celebrated (see no. 178), the second form of the funeral liturgy is used. When the funeral liturgy is celebrated outside Mass before the committal, a Mass for the deceased should be scheduled, if possible, for the family and friends at a convenient time after the funeral.

129 At the funeral liturgy the community gathers with the family and friends of the deceased to give praise and thanks to God for Christ's victory over sin and death, to commend the deceased to God's tender mercy and compassion, and to seek strength in the proclamation of the paschal mystery. Through the Holy Spirit the community is joined together in faith as one Body in Christ to reaffirm in sign and symbol, word and gesture that each believer through baptism shares in Christ's death and resurrection and can look to the day when all the elect will be raised up and united in the kingdom of light and peace.

STRUCTURE AND CONTENT OF THE FUNERAL LITURGY

130 The funeral Mass includes the reception of the body, if this has not already occurred, the celebration of the liturgy of the word, the liturgy of the eucharist, and the final commendation and farewell. The funeral liturgy outside Mass includes all these elements except the liturgy of the eucharist. Both the funeral

Mass and the funeral liturgy outside Mass may be followed by the procession to the place of committal.

RECEPTION AT THE CHURCH

131 Since the church is the place where the community of faith assembles for worship, the rite of reception of the body at the church has great significance. The church is the place where the Christian life is begotten in baptism, nourished in the eucharist, and where the community gathers to commend one of its deceased members to the Father. The church is at once a symbol of the community and of the heavenly liturgy that the celebration of the liturgy anticipates. In the act of receiving the body, the members of the community acknowledge the deceased as one of their own, as one who was welcomed in baptism and who held a place in the assembly. Through the use of various baptismal symbols the community shows the reverence due to the body, the temple of the Spirit, and in this way prepares for the funeral liturgy in which it asks for a share in the heavenly banquet promised to the deceased and to all who have been washed in the waters of rebirth and marked with the sign of faith.

132 Any national flags or the flags or insignia of associations to which the deceased belonged are to be removed from the coffin at the entrance to the church. They may be replaced after the coffin has been taken from the church.

133 The rite of reception takes place at the beginning of the funeral liturgy, usually at the entrance of the church. It begins with a greeting of the family and others who have accompanied the coffin to the door of the church. The minister sprinkles the coffin with holy water in remembrance of the deceased person's initiation and first acceptance into the community of faith. A funeral pall, reminder of the garment given at baptism, and therefore signifying life in Christ, may then be placed on the coffin by family members, friends, or the minister. The entrance procession follows. The minister precedes the coffin and the mourners into the church. If the Easter candle is used on this occasion, it may either be carried before the coffin in the entrance procession or placed beforehand near the position the coffin will occupy at the conclusion of the procession.

134 If in this rite a symbol of the Christian life is to be placed on the coffin, it is carried in the procession and is placed on the coffin by a family member, friend, or the minister at the conclusion of the procession.

135 To draw the community together in prayer at the beginning of the funeral liturgy, the procession should be accompanied, whenever possible, by the singing of the entrance song. This song ought to be a profound expression of belief in eternal life and the resurrection of the dead as well as a prayer of intercession for the deceased (see, for example, no. 403).

136 If the rite of reception has already taken place, the funeral Mass begins in the usual way and the funeral liturgy outside Mass begins with the entrance song, followed by the greeting and an invitation to prayer.

LITURGY OF THE WORD

137 The reading of the word of God is an essential element of the celebration of the funeral liturgy. The readings proclaim the paschal mystery, teach remembrance of the dead, convey the hope of being gathered together again in God's kingdom, and encourage the witness of Christian life. Above all, the readings tell of God's design for a world in which suffering and death will relinquish their hold on all whom God has called his own.

138 Depending on pastoral circumstances, there may be either one or two readings before the gospel reading. When there is a first and second reading before the gospel reading, it is preferable to have a different reader for each.

139 The responsorial psalm enables the community to respond in faith to the first reading. Through the psalms the community expresses its grief and praise, and acknowledges its Creator and Redeemer as the sure source of trust and hope in times of trial. Since the responsorial psalm is a song, whenever possible, it should be sung. Psalms may be sung responsorially, with the response sung by the assembly and all the verses by the cantor or choir, or directly, with no response and all the verses sung by all or by the cantor or choir. When not sung, the responsorial psalm after the reading should be recited in a manner conducive to meditation on the word of God.[1]

140 In the *alleluia,* or the gospel acclamation, the community welcomes the Lord who is about to speak to it. If the *alleluia* is not sung, it is omitted. The cantor or choir sings the *alleluia* or Lenten acclamation first and the people repeat it. The verse is then sung by the cantor or choir and the *alleluia* or Lenten acclamation is then sung once more by all.

141 A brief homily based on the readings should always be given at the funeral liturgy, but never any kind of eulogy. The homilist should dwell on God's compassionate love and on the paschal mystery of the Lord as proclaimed in the Scripture readings. Through the homily, the community should receive the consolation and strength to face the death of one of its members with a hope that has been nourished by the proclamation of the saving word of God.

142 In the intercessions the community responds to the proclamation of the word of God by prayer for the deceased and all the dead, for the bereaved and all who mourn, and for all in the assembly. The intercessions provided may be used or adapted to the circumstances, or new intercessions may be composed.

---

[1] See Lectionary for Mass (2nd *editio typica,* 1981), General Introduction, no. 22.

LITURGY OF THE EUCHARIST

143 At the funeral Mass, the community, having been spiritually renewed at the table of God's word, turns for spiritual nourishment to the table of the eucharist. The community with the priest offers to the Father the sacrifice of the New Covenant and shares in the one bread and the one cup. In partaking of the body of Christ, all are given a foretaste of eternal life in Christ and are united with Christ, with each other, and with all the faithful, living and dead: "Because there is one bread, we who are many are one body, for we all partake of the one bread" (1 Corinthians 10:17).

144 The liturgy of the eucharist takes place in the usual manner at the funeral Mass. Members of the family or friends of the deceased should bring the gifts to the altar. Instrumental music or a song (for example, Psalm 18:1-6, Psalm 63, Psalm 66:13-20, or Psalm 138) may accompany the procession with the gifts. Before the priest washes his hands, he may incense the gifts and the altar. Afterward the deacon or other minister may incense the priest and the congregation.

Eucharistic Prayer II and Eucharistic Prayer III are especially appropriate for use at the funeral Mass, because they provide special texts of intercession for the dead. Since music gives greater solemnity to a ritual action, the singing of the people's parts of the eucharistic prayer should be encouraged, that is, the responses of the preface dialogue, the Sanctus, the memorial acclamation, and the Great Amen.

To reinforce and to express more fully the unity of the congregation during the communion rite, the people may sing the Lord's Prayer, the doxology, the Lamb of God, and a song for the communion procession (for example, Psalm 23, Psalm 27, Psalm 34, Psalm 63, or Psalm 121).

FINAL COMMENDATION AND FAREWELL

145 At the conclusion of the funeral liturgy, the rite of final commendation and farewell is celebrated, unless it is to be celebrated later at the place of committal.

146 The final commendation is a final farewell by the members of the community, an act of respect for one of their members, whom they entrust to the tender and merciful embrace of God. This act of last farewell also acknowledges the reality of separation and affirms that the community and the deceased, baptized into the one Body, share the same destiny, resurrection on the last day. On that day the one Shepherd will call each by name and gather the faithful together in the new and eternal Jerusalem.

147 The rite begins with the minister's opening words and a few moments of silent prayer. The opening words serve as a brief explanation of the rite and as an invitation to pray in silence for the deceased. The pause for silence

allows the bereaved and all present to relate their own feelings of loss and grief to the mystery of Christian hope in God's abundant mercy and his promise of eternal life.

Where this is customary, the body may then be sprinkled with holy water and incensed, or this may be done during or after the song of farewell. The sprinkling is a reminder that through baptism the person was marked for eternal life and the incensation signifies respect for the body as the temple of the Holy Spirit.

The song of farewell, which should affirm hope and trust in the paschal mystery, is the climax of the rite of final commendation. It should be sung to a melody simple enough for all to sing. It may take the form of a responsory or even a hymn. When singing is not possible, invocations may be recited by the assembly.

A prayer of commendation concludes the rite. In this prayer the community calls upon God's mercy, commends the deceased into God's hands, and affirms its belief that those who have died in Christ will share in Christ's victory over death.

PROCESSION TO THE PLACE OF COMMITTAL

148 At the conclusion of the funeral liturgy, the procession is formed and the body is accompanied to the place of committal. This final procession of the funeral rite mirrors the journey of human life as a pilgrimage to God's kingdom of peace and light, the new and eternal Jerusalem.

149 Especially when accompanied with music and singing, the procession can help to reinforce the bond of communion between the participants. Whenever possible, psalms or songs may accompany the entire procession from the church to the place of committal. In situations where a solemn procession on foot from the church to the place of committal is not possible, an antiphon or song may be sung as the body is being taken to the entrance of the church. Psalms, hymns, or liturgical songs may also be sung by the participants as they gather at the place of committal.

MINISTRY AND PARTICIPATION

150 Because the funeral liturgy is the central celebration for the deceased, it should be scheduled for a time that permits as many of the Christian community as possible to be present. The full and active participation of the assembly affirms the value of praying for the dead, gives strength and support to the bereaved, and is a sure sign of faith and hope in the paschal mystery. Every

effort, therefore, should be made by the various liturgical ministers to encourage the active participation of the family and of the entire assembly.

151 The priest is the ordinary presiding minister of the funeral liturgy. Except for Mass, a deacon may conduct the funeral liturgy. If pastoral need requires, the conference of bishops, with the permission of the Apostolic See, may decide that laypersons also preside at the funeral liturgy outside Mass.

152 Whenever possible, ministers should involve the family in the planning of the funeral liturgy: in the choice of readings, prayers, and music for the liturgy and in the designation of ushers, pallbearers, readers, acolytes, special ministers of the eucharist, when needed, and musicians. The family should also be given the opportunity to designate persons who will place the pall or other Christian symbols on the coffin during the rite of reception of the body at the church and who will bring the gifts to the altar at Mass.

153 An organist or other instrumentalist, a cantor, and, whenever possible, a choir should be present to assist the congregation in singing the songs, responses, and acclamations of the funeral liturgy.

FUNERAL MASS

Until the Lord comes, you are proclaiming his death

154 When one of its members dies, the Church encourages the celebration of the Mass. In the proclamation of the Scriptures, the saving word of God through the power of the Spirit becomes living and active in the minds and hearts of the community. Having been strengthened at the table of God's word, the community calls to mind God's saving deeds and offers the Father in the Spirit the eucharistic sacrifice of Christ's Passover from death to life, a living sacrifice of praise and thanksgiving, of reconciliation and atonement. Communion nourishes the community and expresses its unity. In communion, the participants have a foretaste of the heavenly banquet that awaits them and are reminded of Christ's own words: "Whoever eats my flesh and drinks my blood shall live for ever" (John 6:55). Confident in Jesus' presence among them in the living word, the living sacrifice, the living meal, those present in union with the whole Church offer prayers and petitions for the deceased, whom they entrust to God's merciful love.

155 The funeral Mass is ordinarily celebrated in the parish church.

156 The Mass texts are those of the Roman Missal and the Lectionary for Mass, "Masses for the Dead." The intercessions should be adapted to the circumstances. Models are given in place and in Part V, no. 401.

157 In the choice of music for the funeral Mass, preference should be given to the singing of the acclamations, the responsorial psalm, the entrance and communion songs, and especially the song of farewell at the final commendation.

FUNERAL LITURGY OUTSIDE MASS

I am the resurrection and the life; whoever believes in me shall never die

177 In the funeral liturgy outside Mass the community gathers to hear the message of Easter hope proclaimed in the liturgy of the word and to commend the deceased to God.

178 This rite may be used for various reasons:

1. when the funeral Mass is not permitted, namely, on solemnities of obligation, on Holy Thursday and the Easter Triduum, and on the Sundays of Advent, Lent, and the Easter Season;[1]
2. when in some places or circumstances it is not possible to celebrate the funeral Mass before the committal, for example, if a priest is not available;
3. when for pastoral reasons the pastor and the family judge that the funeral liturgy outside Mass is a more suitable form of celebration.

179 The funeral liturgy outside Mass is ordinarily celebrated in the parish church, but may also be celebrated in the home of the deceased, a funeral home, parlor, chapel of rest, or cemetery chapel.

180 The readings are those of the Lectionary for Mass, "Masses for the Dead." The intercessions should be adapted to the circumstances. Models are given in place and in Part V, no. 401. The celebration may also include holy communion.

181 In the choice of music for the funeral liturgy, preference should be given to the singing of the entrance song, the responsorial psalm, the gospel acclamation, and especially the song of farewell at the final commendation.

182 The minister who is a priest or deacon wears an alb with stole (a cope may be used, if desired); a layperson who presides wears the liturgical vestments approved for the region.

---

[1] See General Instruction of the Roman Missal, no. 336.

RITE OF COMMITTAL

Joseph took Jesus down from the cross,
wrapped him in a shroud,
and laid him in a tomb

204 The rite of committal, the conclusion of the funeral rites, is the final act of the community of faith in caring for the body of its deceased member. It may be celebrated at the grave, tomb, or crematorium and may be used for burial at sea. Whenever possible, the rite of committal is to be celebrated at the site of committal, that is, beside the open grave or place of interment, rather than at a cemetery chapel.

205 Two forms of the rite of committal are provided here: "Rite of Committal" and "Rite of Committal with Final Commendation." The first form is used when the final commendation is celebrated as part of the conclusion of the funeral liturgy. The second form is used when the final commendation does not take place during the funeral liturgy or when no funeral liturgy precedes the committal rite.

206 In committing the body to its resting place, the community expresses the hope that, with all those who have gone before marked with the sign of faith, the deceased awaits the glory of the resurrection. The rite of committal is an expression of the communion that exists between the Church on earth and the Church in heaven: the deceased passes with the farewell prayers of the community of believers into the welcoming company of those who need faith no longer but see God face to face.

STRUCTURE AND CONTENT OF THE RITE OF COMMITTAL

207 Both forms of the committal rite begin with an invitation, Scripture verse, and a prayer over the place of committal. The several alternatives for the

prayer over the place of committal take into account whether the grave, tomb, or resting place has already been blessed and situations in which the final disposition of the body will actually take place at a later time (for example, when the body is to be cremated or will remain in a cemetery chapel until burial at a later time).

208 The rite of committal continues with the words of committal, the intercessions, and the Lord's Prayer.

The rite of committal with final commendation continues with an invitation to prayer, a pause for silent prayer, the sprinkling and incensing of the body, where this is customary, the song of farewell, and the prayer of commendation (see nos. 227-231).

209 The act of committal takes place after the words of committal (in the rite of committal with final commendation, after the prayer of commendation) or at the conclusion of the rite. The act of committal expresses the full significance of this rite. Through this act the community of faith proclaims that the grave or place of interment, once a sign of futility and despair, has been transformed by means of Christ's own death and resurrection into a sign of hope and promise.

210 Both forms of the rite conclude with a prayer over the people, which includes the verse *Eternal rest,* and a blessing. Depending on local custom, a song may then be sung and a gesture of final leave-taking may be made, for example, placing flowers or soil on the coffin.

ADAPTATION

211 If there is pastoral need for a longer committal rite than those provided here, for example, when the funeral liturgy has been celebrated on a previous day or in a different community, the minister may use the appropriate form of the committal rite and adapt it, for example, by adding a greeting, song, one or more readings, a psalm, and a brief homily. When there has been no funeral liturgy prior to the committal rite, the "Rite of Committal with Final Commendation" may be used and similarly adapted.

212 The rite of committal may be celebrated in circumstances in which the final disposition of the body will not take place for some time, for example, when winter delays burial or when ashes are to be interred at some time after cremation. The rite of committal may then be repeated on the later occasion when the actual burial or interment takes place. On the second occasion the rite may include a longer Scripture reading as well as a homily.

In the case of a body donated to science, the rite of committal may be celebrated whenever interment takes place.

MINISTRY AND PARTICIPATION

213 The community continues to show its concern for the mourners by participating in the rite of committal. The rite marks the separation in this life of the mourners from the deceased, and through it the community assists them as they complete their care for the deceased and lay the body to rest. When carried out in the midst of the community of faith, the committal can help the mourners to face the end of one relationship with the deceased and to begin a new one based on prayerful remembrance, gratitude, and the hope of resurrection and reunion.

By their presence and prayer members of the community signify their intention to continue to support the mourners in the time following the funeral.

214 The singing of well-chosen music at the rite of committal can help the mourners as they face the reality of the separation. At the rite of committal with final commendation, whenever possible, the song of farewell should be sung. In either form of the committal rite, a hymn or liturgical song that affirms hope in God's mercy and in the resurrection of the dead is desirable at the conclusion of the rite.

215 In the absence of a parish minister, a friend or member of the family should lead those present in the rite of committal.

The minister should vest according to local custom.

PART II
FUNERAL RITES
FOR CHILDREN

Let the little children come to me;
it is to such as these that the kingdom of God belongs

234 Part II of the *Order of Christian Funerals* provides rites that are used in the funerals of infants and young children, including those of early school age. It includes "Vigil for a Deceased Child," "Funeral Liturgy," and "Rite of Committal."

Part II does not contain "Related Rites and Prayers," nos. 98-127, which are brief rites for prayer with the family and friends before the funeral liturgy. The rites as they are presented in Part I are models and should be adapted by the minister to the circumstances of the funeral for a child.

235 The minister, in consultation with those concerned, chooses those rites that best correspond to the particular needs and customs of the mourners. In some instances, for example, the death of an infant, only the rite of committal and perhaps one of the forms of prayer with the family may be desirable.

236 In the celebration of the funeral of a child the Church offers worship to God, the author of life, commends the child to God's love, and prays for the consolation of the family and close friends.

237 Funeral rites may be celebrated for children whose parents intended them to be baptized but who died before baptism.[1] In these celebrations the Christian community entrusts the child to God's all-embracing love and finds strength in this love and in Jesus' affirmation that the kingdom of God belongs to little children (see Matthew 19:14).

---

[1] In the general catechesis of the faithful, pastors and other ministers should explain that the celebration of the funeral rites for children who die before baptism is not intended to weaken the Church's teaching on the necessity of baptism.

238 In its pastoral ministry to the bereaved the Christian community is challenged in a particular way by the death of an infant or child. The bewilderment and pain that death causes can be overwhelming in this situation, especially for the parents and the brothers and sisters of the deceased child. The community seeks to offer support and consolation to the family during and after the time of the funeral rites.

239 Through prayer and words of comfort the minister and others can help the mourners to understand that their child has gone before them into the kingdom of the Lord and that one day they will all be reunited there in joy. The participation of the community in the funeral rites is a sign of the compassionate presence of Christ, who embraced little children, wept at the death of a friend, and endured the pain and separation of death in order to render it powerless over those he loves. Christ still sorrows with those who sorrow and longs with them for the fulfillment of the Father's plan in a new creation where tears and death will have no place.

240 The minister should invite members of the community to use their individual gifts in this ministry of consolation. Those who have lost children of their own may be able in a special way to help the family as they struggle to accept the death of the child.

241 Those involved in planning the funeral rites for a deceased child should take into account the age of the child, the circumstances of death, the grief of the family, and the needs and customs of those taking part in the rites. In choosing the texts and elements of celebration, the minister should bear in mind whether the child was baptized or died before baptism.

242 Special consideration should be given to any sisters, brothers, friends, or classmates of the deceased child who may be present at the funeral rites. Children will be better able to take part in the celebration if the various elements are planned and selected with them in mind: texts, readings, music, gesture, processions, silence. The minister may wish to offer brief remarks for the children's benefit at suitable points during the celebration.

If children will be present at the funeral rites, those with requisite ability should be asked to exercise some of the liturgical roles. During the funeral Mass, for example, children may serve as readers, acolytes, or musicians, or assist in the reading of the general intercessions and in the procession with the gifts. Depending upon the age and number of children taking part, adaptations recommended in the *Directory for Masses with Children* may be appropriate.

VIGIL

It is good to wait in silence for the Lord

VIGIL FOR A DECEASED CHILD

243 The vigil for the deceased is the principal celebration of the Christian community during the time before the funeral liturgy or, if there is no funeral liturgy, before the rite of committal. The vigil may take the form of a liturgy of the word, as described in Part I, nos. 57-68, or of some part of the office for the dead (see Part IV, nos. 348-395).

244 The vigil may be celebrated at a convenient time in the home of the deceased child, in the funeral home, parlor or chapel of rest, or in some other suitable place. The vigil may also be celebrated in the church, but at a time well before the funeral liturgy, so that the funeral liturgy will not be lengthy and liturgy of the word repetitious. When the body is brought to the church for the celebration of the vigil, the vigil begins with the rite of reception (see no. 58). Otherwise the vigil begins with a greeting, followed by an opening song, an invitation to prayer, and an opening prayer.

245 After the opening prayer, the vigil continues with the liturgy of the word, which usually includes a first reading, responsorial psalm, gospel reading, and homily. If there is to be only one reading, however, it should be the gospel reading. The prayer of intercession, which includes a litany, the Lord's Prayer, and a concluding prayer, then follows. Alternative concluding prayers are provided for use in the case of a baptized child or of a child who died before baptism. The vigil concludes with a blessing, which may be followed by a song or a few moments of silent prayer or both.

246 The minister should adapt the vigil to the circumstances. If, for example, a large number of children are present or if the vigil is held in the home of

the deceased child, elements of the rite may be simplified or shortened and other elements or symbols that have special meaning for those taking part may be incorporated into the celebration. If custom and circumstances suggest, a member or a friend of the family may speak in remembrance of the deceased child.

FUNERAL LITURGY

The Lord will wipe away the tears from every cheek

264 The funeral liturgy, as described in nos. 128-153, is the central liturgical celebration of the Christian community for the deceased. Two forms of the funeral liturgy are provided: "Funeral Mass" and "Funeral Liturgy outside Mass." If the second form is used, Mass may be celebrated at a later date.

265 The funeral Mass includes the reception of the body, if this has not already occurred, the celebration of the liturgy of the word, the liturgy of the eucharist, and the final commendation and farewell. The funeral liturgy outside Mass includes all these elements except the liturgy of the eucharist. Both the funeral Mass and the funeral liturgy outside Mass may be followed by the procession to the place of committal.

266 The rite of reception of the body begins with a greeting of the family and others who have accompanied the body to the door of the church. The minister may give brief explanations of the symbols in this rite for the benefit of any children who may be present for the celebration. In the case of a baptized child, the minister sprinkles the coffin in remembrance of the deceased child's acceptance into the community of faith. A funeral pall, reminder of the garment given at baptism and therefore signifying life in Christ, may then be placed on the coffin by family members, friends, or the minister. In the case of a child who died before baptism, the minister addresses the community with a few words. The entrance procession follows. The minister precedes the coffin and the mourners into the church, as all sing an entrance song. The Easter candle may be carried before the coffin in the entrance procession or placed beforehand near the position the coffin will occupy at the conclusion of the procession.

If in this rite a symbol of the Christian life is to be placed on the coffin, it is carried in the procession and is placed on the coffin by a family member, friend, or the minister at the conclusion of the procession.

267 The rite of final commendation and farewell is celebrated at the conclusion of the funeral liturgy unless it is deferred for celebration at the place of

committal. The rite begins with the invitation to prayer, followed by a pause for silent prayer. In the case of a baptized child, the body may then be sprinkled with holy water and incensed. Or this may be done during or after the song of farewell. The song of farewell is then sung and the rite concludes with the prayer of commendation.

FUNERAL MASS

268 The funeral Mass is ordinarily celebrated in the parish church, but, at the discretion of the local Ordinary, it may be celebrated in the home of the deceased child or some other place.

269 The Mass texts are those of the Roman Missal and the Lectionary for Mass, "Masses for the Dead." The intercessions should be adapted to the circumstances; models are given in place and in Part V, no. 401.

270 In the choice of music for the funeral Mass, preference should be given to the singing of the acclamations, the responsorial psalm, the entrance and communion songs, and especially the song of farewell at the final commendation.

FUNERAL LITURGY OUTSIDE MASS

271 The funeral liturgy outside Mass may be celebrated for various reasons:
1. when the funeral Mass is not permitted, namely, on solemnities of obligation, on Holy Thursday and the Easter Triduum, and on the Sundays of Advent, Lent, and the Easter season;[1]
2. when in some places or circumstances it is not possible to celebrate the funeral Mass before the committal, for example, if a priest is not available;
3. when for pastoral reasons pastor and the family decide that the funeral liturgy outside Mass is a more suitable form of celebration for the deceased child.

272 The funeral liturgy outside Mass is ordinarily celebrated in the parish church, but may also be celebrated in the home of the deceased, a funeral home, parlor, chapel of rest, or cemetery chapel.

273 The readings are those of the Lectionary for Mass, "Masses for the Dead." The intercessions should be adapted to the circumstances; models are given in place and in Part V, no. 401. The celebration may include holy communion.

---

[1] See General Instruction of the Roman Missal, no. 336.

274 In the choice of music for the funeral liturgy, preference should be given to the singing of the entrance song, the responsorial psalm, the gospel acclamation, and especially the song of farewell at the final commendation.
275 The minister who is a priest or deacon wears an alb or surplice with stole (a cope may be used, if desired); a layperson who presides wears the liturgical vestments approved for the region.

RITE OF COMMITTAL

The Lord is my shepherd;
fresh and green are the pastures
where he gives me repose

316 The rite of committal, the conclusion of the funeral rites (see nos. 204-215), is celebrated at the grave, tomb, or crematorium and may be used for burial at sea.

Three forms of the rite of committal are provided for the funeral of a child: "Rite of Committal," "Rite of Committal with Final Commendation," and "Rite of Final Commendation for an Infant."

317 The rite of committal is used when the final commendation and farewell is celebrated within the funeral liturgy. The rite of committal with final commendation is used when the final commendation is not celebrated within the funeral liturgy.

When the funeral liturgy is celebrated on a day prior to the committal or in a different community, the minister may wish to adapt the rite of committal, for example, by adding a song, a greeting, one or more readings, a psalm, and a brief homily. When no funeral liturgy precedes the rite of committal, the rite of committal with final commendation is used and should be similarly adapted.

318 The "Rite of Final Commendation for an Infant" may be used in the case of a stillborn or a newborn infant who dies shortly after birth. This short rite of prayer with the parents is celebrated to give them comfort and to commend and entrust the infant to God. This rite is a model and the minister should adapt it to the circumstances. It may be used in the hospital or place of birth or at the time of the committal of the body.

PART III
TEXTS OF SACRED SCRIPTURE

We shall not live on bread alone,
but on every word that comes from God

343 Part III, "Texts of Sacred Scripture," contains the Scriptural readings and psalms for the celebration of the funeral. It is divided into four sections: "Funerals for Adults," "Funerals for Baptized Children," "Funerals for Children Who Died before Baptism," "Antiphons and Psalms."

344 As a general rule, all corresponding texts from sacred Scripture in the funeral rites are interchangeable. In consultation with the family and close friends, the minister chooses the texts that most closely reflect the particular circumstances and the needs of the mourners.

PART IV
OFFICE FOR THE DEAD

With the Lord there is mercy
and fullness of redemption

348 The vigil for the deceased may be celebrated in the form of some part of the office for the dead. To encourage this form of the vigil, the chief hours, "Morning Prayer" and "Evening Prayer" are provided here. When the funeral liturgy is celebrated the evening before the committal, it may be appropriate to celebrate morning prayer before the procession to the place of committal.
349 In the celebration of the office for the dead members of the Christian community gather to offer praise and thanks to God especially for the gifts of redemption and resurrection, to intecede for the dead, and to find strength in Christ's victory over death. When the community celebrates the hours, Christ the Mediator and High Priest is truly present through his Spirit in the gathered assembly, in the proclamation of God's word, and in the prayer and song of the Church.[1] The community's celebration of the hours acknowledges that spiritual bond that links the Church on earth with the Church in heaven, for it is in union with the whole Church that this prayer is offered on behalf of the deceased.
350 At morning prayer the Christian community recalls "the resurrection of the Lord Jesus, the true light enlightening all people (see John 1:9) and 'the sun of justice' (Malachi 4:2) 'rising from on high' (Luke 1:78)."[2] The celebration of morning prayer from the office for the dead relates the death of the Christian to Christ's victory over death and affirms the hope that those who have received the light of Christ at baptism, will share in that victory.
351 At evening prayer the Christian community gathers to give thanks for the gifts it has received, to recall the sacrifice of Jesus Christ and the saving works

---

[1] See General Instruction of the Liturgy of the Hours, no. 13.
[2] See General Instruction of the Liturgy of the Hours, no. 38.

of redemption, and to call upon Christ, the evening star and unconquerable light.[3] Through evening prayer from the office for the dead the community gives thanks to God for the gift of life received by the deceased and praises the Father for the redemption brought about by the sacrifice of his Son, who is the joy-giving light and the true source of hope.

STRUCTURE AND CONTENT OF MORNING PRAYER AND EVENING PRAYER

352 Morning prayer and evening prayer from the office for the dead include the introduction (or the reception of the body), hymn, psalmody, reading, response to the word of God, gospel canticle, intercessions, concluding prayer, and dismissal.

INTRODUCTORY VERSE OR RECEPTION OF THE BODY

353 Morning prayer and evening prayer begin with the introductory verse, *God, come to my assistance,* except when the invitatory replaces it, or when the rite of reception of the body is celebrated, since this replaces both the introductory verse and the hymn.

HYMN

354 To set the tone for the hour, a hymn is sung.

PSALMODY

355 In praying the psalms of the office for the dead, the assembly offers God praise and intercedes for the deceased person and the mourners in the words of prayer that Jesus himself used during his life on earth. Through the psalms the assembly prays in the voice of Christ, who intercedes on its behalf before the Father. In the psalms of petition and lament it expresses its sorrow and its firm hope in the redemption won by Christ. In the psalms of praise the assembly has a foretaste of the destiny of its deceased member and its own destiny, participation in the liturgy of heaven, where every tear will be wiped away and the Lord's victory over death will be complete.

---

[3] See General Instruction of the Liturgy of the Hours, no. 39.

356 Since the psalms are songs, whenever possible, they should be sung. The manner of singing them may be:

1. antiphonal, that is, two groups alternate singing the stanzas; the last stanza, the doxology, is sung by both groups;
2. responsorial, that is, the antiphon is sung by all before and after each stanza and the stanzas are sung by a cantor;
3. direct, that is, the stanzas are sung without interruption by all, by a choir, or by a cantor.

The rubrics for each psalm in morning prayer and evening prayer indicate a way for singing it; other ways may be used.

357 The psalmody of morning prayer from the office for the dead consists of Psalm 51, a psalm of lament and petition, Psalm 146 or Psalm 150, a psalm of praise, and an Old Testament canticle from Isaiah.

358 The psalmody of evening prayer consists of Psalm 121 and Psalm 130, two psalms of lament and petition, and a New Testament canticle from the letter of Paul to the Philippians.

359 For pastoral reasons, psalms other than those given in the office for the dead may be chosen, provided they are appropriate for the time of day and suitable for use in the office for the dead (see, for example, antiphons and psalms in Part III).[4]

READING

360 The reading of the word of God in the office for the dead proclaims the paschal mystery and conveys the hope of being gathered together again in God's kingdom. The short reading in place in the hour or a longer Scripture reading from Part III may be used.[5] For pastoral reasons and if circumstances allow, a nonbiblical reading may be included at morning or evening prayer in addition to the reading from Scripture, as is the practice in the office of readings.

RESPONSE TO THE WORD OF GOD

361 A period of silence may follow the reading, then a brief homily based on the reading. After the homily the short responsory or another responsorial song may be sung or recited.

---

[4] See General Instruction of the Liturgy of the Hours, no. 252.
[5] See General Instruction of the Liturgy of the Hours, no. 46.

GOSPEL CANTICLE

362 After the response to the word of God, the Canticle of Zechariah is sung at morning prayer and the Canticle of Mary at evening prayer as an expression of praise and thanksgiving for redemption.[6]

363 During the singing of the gospel canticle, the altar, then the presiding minister and the congregation may be incensed.

INTERCESSIONS

364 In the intercessions of the office for the dead, the assembly prays that the deceased and all who die marked with the sign of faith may rise again together in glory with Christ. The intercessions provided in the hour may be used or adapted to the circumstances, or new intercessions may be composed.

The presiding minister introduces the intercessions. An assisting minister sings or says the intentions. In keeping with the form of the intentions in the liturgy of the hours, the assembly responds with either the second part of the intention or the response. After a brief introduction by the presiding minister the assembly sings or says the Lord's Prayer.

CONCLUDING PRAYER AND DISMISSAL

365 The concluding prayer, proclaimed by the presiding minister, completes the hour.

366 After the concluding prayer and before the dismissal a member of the family or a friend of the deceased may be invited to speak in remembrance of the deceased.

367 When the funeral liturgy is celebrated the evening before the committal, it may be appropriate to celebrate morning prayer before the procession to the place of committal. In such an instance the dismissal is omitted and the rite continues with the procession to the place of committal.

MINISTRY AND PARTICIPATION

368 The celebration of the office for the dead requires careful preparation, especially in the case of communities that may not be familiar with the liturgy of the hours. Pastors and other ministers should provide catechesis on the

---

[6] See General Instruction of the Liturgy of the Hours, no. 50.

place and significance of the liturgy of the hours in the life of the Church and the purpose of the celebration of the office for the dead. They should also encourage members of the parish community to participate in the celebration as an effective means of prayer for the deceased, as a sign of their concern and support for the family and close friends, and as a sign of faith and hope in the paschal mystery. This catechesis will help to ensure the full and active participation of the assembly in the celebration of the office for the dead.

369 The office for the dead may be celebrated in the funeral home, parlor, chapel of rest, or in the church. In special circumstances, when the office is combined with the funeral liturgy, care should be taken that the celebration not be too lengthy.[7]

370 The place in which the celebration occurs will often suggest adaptations. A celebration in the home of the deceased, for example, may be simplified or shortened.

371 A priest or deacon should normally preside whenever the office for the dead is celebrated with a congregation; other ministers (a reader, a cantor, an acolyte) should exercise their proper ministries. In the absence of a priest or deacon, a layperson presides.

Whenever possible, ministers should involve the family of the deceased in the planning of the hour and in the designation of ministers.

The minister vests according to local custom. If morning prayer or evening prayer is celebrated in the church, a priest or a deacon who presides wears an alb or surplice with stole (a cope may also be worn).

372 The sung celebration of the liturgy of the hours "is more in keeping with the nature of this prayer, and a mark of both higher solemnity and closer union of hearts in offering praise to God."[8] Whenever possible, therefore, singing at morning or evening prayer should be encouraged.

In the choice of music preference should be given to the singing of the hymn, the psalmody, and the gospel canticle. The introductory verse, the responsory, the intercessions, the Lord's Prayer, and the dismissal may also be sung.

An organist or other instrumentalist and a cantor should assist the assembly in singing the hymn, psalms, and responses. The parish community should also prepare booklets or participation aids that contain an outline of the hour, the texts and music belonging to the people, and directions for posture, gesture, and movement.

[7] See General Instruction of the Liturgy of the Hours, nos. 93-97.
[8] Congregation of Rites, Introduction *Musicam Sacram,* 5 March 1967, no. 37: AAS 59 (1967), 310; DOL 508, no. 4158.

APPENDIX I

INTRODUCTION TO THE
1969 *ORDO EXSEQUIARUM**

1   At the funerals of its children the Church confidently celebrates Christ's paschal mystery. Its intention is that those who by baptism were made one body with the dead and risen Christ may with him pass from death to life. In soul they are to be cleansed and taken up into heaven with the saints and elect; in body they await the blessed hope of Christ's coming and the resurrection of the dead.

The Church, therefore, offers the eucharistic sacrifice of Christ's Passover for the dead and pours forth prayers and petitions for them. Because of the communion of all Christ's members with each other, all of this brings spiritual aid to the dead and the consolation of hope to the living.

2   As they celebrate the funerals of their brothers and sisters, Christians should be intent on affirming their hope for eternal life. They should not, however, give the impression of either disregard or contempt for the attitudes or practices of their own time and place. In such matters as family traditions, local customs, burial societies, Christians should willingly acknowledge whatever they perceive to be good and try to transform whatever seems alien to the Gospel. Then the funeral ceremonies for Christians will both manifest paschal faith and be true examples of the spirit of the Gospel.

3   Although any form of empty display must be excluded, it is right to show respect for the bodies of the faithful departed, which in life were the temple of the Holy Spirit. This is why it is worthwhile that there be an expression of faith in eternal life and the offering of prayers for the deceased, at least at the more significant times between death and burial.

Depending on local custom, such special moments include the vigil at the home of the deceased, the laying out of the body, and the carrying of the body to the place of burial. They should be marked by the gathering of family and friends and, if possible, of the whole community to receive in the liturgy of the word the consolation of hope, to offer together the eucharistic sacrifice, and to pay last respects to the deceased by a final farewell.

4   To take into account in some degree conditions in all parts of the world, the present rite of funerals is arranged on the basis of three models:

---

* As emended by the Congregation for the Sacraments and Divine Worship, 12 September 1983.

1. The first envisions three stations, namely, at the home of the deceased, at the church, and at the cemetery.
2. The second covers only two stations, at the church and at the cemetery.
3. The third involves only one station, which is at the home of the deceased.

5   The first model for a funeral is practically the same as the former rite in the Roman Ritual. It includes as a rule, at least in country places, three stations, namely, at the home of the deceased, at the church, and at the cemetery, with two processions in between. Especially in large cities, however, processions are seldom held or are inconvenient for various reasons. As for the stations at home and at the cemetery, priests sometimes are unable to lead them because of a shortage of clergy or the distance of the cemetery from the church. In view of these considerations, the faithful must be urged to recite the usual psalms and prayers themselves where there is no deacon or priest present. If that is impossible, the home and cemetery stations are to be omitted.

6   In this first model the station at the church consists as a rule in the celebration of the funeral Mass; this is forbidden only during the Easter triduum, on solemnities, and on the Sundays of Advent, Lent, and the Easter season. Pastoral reasons may on occasion require that a funeral be celebrated in the church without a Mass (which in all cases must, if possible, be celebrated on another day within a reasonable time); in that case a liturgy of the word is prescribed absolutely. Therefore, the station at the church always includes a liturgy of the word, with or without a Mass, and the rite hitherto called "absolution" of the dead and henceforth to be called "the final commendation and farewell."

7   The second funeral plan consists of only two stations, namely, at the cemetery, that is, at the cemetery chapel, and at the grave. This plan does not envision a eucharistic celebration, but one is to take place, without the body present, before the actual funeral or after the funeral.

8   A funeral rite, following the third model, to be celebrated in the deceased's home may perhaps in some places be regarded as pointless. Yet in certain parts of the world it seems needed. In view of the many diversities, the model purposefully does not go into details. At the same time it seemed advisable at least to set out guidelines so that this plan might share certain elements with the other two, for example, the liturgy of the word and the rite of final commendation or farewell. The detailed directives will be left to the conferences of bishops to settle.

9   In the future preparation of particular rituals conformed to the Roman Ritual, it will be up to the conference of bishops either to keep the three models or to change their arrangement or to omit one or other of them. For it is quite possible that in any particular country one model, for example, the first with its three stations, is the only one in use and as such the one to be kept. Elsewhere all three may be needed. The conference of bishops will make the arrangements appropriate to what particular needs require.

10   After the funeral Mass the rite of final commendation and farewell is celebrated.

The meaning of the rite does not signify a kind of purification of the deceased; that is what the eucharistic sacrifice accomplishes. Rather it stands as a farewell by which the Christian community together pays respect to one of its members before the body is removed or buried. Death, of course, always has involved an element of separation, but Christians as Christ's members are one in him and not even death can part them from each other.[1]

The priest's opening words are to introduce and explain this rite, a few moments of silence are to follow, then the sprinkling with holy water and the incensation, then a song of farewell. Not only is it useful for all to sing this song, composed of a pertinent text set to a suitable melody, but all should have the sense of its being the high point of the entire rite.

Also to be seen as signs of farewell are the sprinkling with holy water, a reminder that through baptism the person was marked for eternal life, and the incensation, signifying respect for the body as the temple of the Holy Spirit.

The rite of final commendation and farewell may only be held during an actual funeral service, that is, when the body is present.

11   In any celebration for the deceased, whether a funeral or not, the rite attaches great importance to the readings from the word of God. These proclaim the paschal mystery, they convey the hope of being gathered together again in God's kingdom, they teach remembrance of the dead, and throughout they encourage the witness of a Christian life.

12   In its good offices on behalf of the dead, the Church turns again and again especially to the prayer of the psalms as an expression of grief and a sure source of trust. Pastors are, therefore, to make an earnest effort through an effective catechesis to lead their communities to a clearer and deeper grasp of at least some of the psalms provided for the funeral liturgy. With regard to other chants that the rite frequently assigns on pastoral grounds, they are also to seek to instill a "warm and living love of Scripture"[2] and a sense of its meaning in the liturgy.

13   In its prayers the Christian community confesses its faith and makes compassionate intercession for deceased adults that they may reach their final happiness with God. The community's belief is that deceased children whom through baptism God has adopted as his own have already attained that blessedness. But the community pours forth its prayers on behalf of their parents, as well as for all the loved ones of the dead, so that in their grief they will experience the comfort of faith.

14   The practice of reciting the office of the dead on the occasion of funerals or at other times is based in some places on particular law, on an endowment for this purpose, or on custom. The practice may be continued, provided the

---

[1]   See Simeon of Thessalonica, *De ordine sepulturae*: PG 155, 685 B.

[2]   Vatican Council II, Constitution on the Liturgy *Sacrosanctum Concilium,* art. 24.

office is celebrated becomingly and devoutly. But in view of the circumstances of contemporary life and for pastoral considerations, a Bible vigil or celebration of God's word may be substituted.

14bis Funeral rites are to be celebrated for catechumens. In keeping with the provisions of CIC, can. 1183, celebration of funeral rites may also be granted to:

1. children whose baptism was intended by their parents but who died before being baptized;
2. baptized members of another Church or non-Catholic Ecclesial Community at the discretion of the local Ordinary, but not if it is known that they did not wish this nor if a minister of their own is available.

15 Funeral rites are to be granted to those who have chosen cremation, unless there is evidence that their choice was dictated by anti-Christian motives.

The funeral is to be celebrated according to the model in use in the region. It should be carried out in a way, however, that clearly expresses the Church's preference for the custom of burying the dead, after the example of Christ's own will to be buried, and that forestalls any danger of scandalizing or shocking the faithful.

The rites usually held in the cemetery chapel or at the grave may in this case take place within the confines of the crematorium and, for want of any other suitable place, even in the crematorium room. Every precaution is to be taken against the danger of scandal or religious indifferentism.

OFFICES AND MINISTRIES TOWARD THE DEAD

16 In the celebration of a funeral all the members of the people of God must remember that to each one a role and an office is entrusted: to relatives and friends, funeral directors, the Christian community as such, finally, the priest, who as the teacher of faith and the minister of comfort presides at the liturgical rites and celebrates the eucharist.

17 All should also be mindful, and priests especially, that as they commend the deceased to God at a funeral, they have a responsibility as well to raise the hopes of those present and to build up their faith in the paschal mystery and the resurrection of the dead. They should do so in such a way, however, that as bearers of the tenderness of the Church and the comfort of faith, they console those who believe without offending those who grieve.

18 In preparing and planning a funeral, priests are to keep in mind with delicate sensitivity not only the identity of the deceased and the circumstances of the death, but also the grief of the bereaved and their needs for a Christian life. Priests are to be particularly mindful of those who attend the liturgical celebration or hear the Gospel because of the funeral, but are either non-

Catholics or Catholics who never or seldom take part in the eucharist or have apparently lost the faith. Priests are, after all, the servants of Christ's Gospel on behalf of all.

19 Except for the Mass, a deacon may conduct all the funeral rites. As pastoral needs require, the conference of bishops, with the Apostolic See's permission, may even depute a layperson for this.

When there is no priest or deacon, it is recommended that in funerals according to the first model laypersons carry out the stations at the home and cemetery; the same applies generally to all vigils for the dead.

20 Apart from the marks of distinction arising from a person's liturgical function or holy orders and those honors due to civil authorities according to liturgical law,[3] no special honors are to be paid in the celebration of a funeral to any private persons or classes of persons.

ADAPTATIONS BELONGING TO THE CONFERENCES OF BISHOPS

21 In virtue of the Constitution on the Liturgy (art. 63 b), the conferences of bishops have the right to prepare a section in particular rituals corresponding to the present section of the Roman Ritual and adapted to the needs of the different parts of the world. This section is for use in the regions concerned, once the *acta* of the conferences have been reviewed by the Apostolic See.

In making such adaptations it shall be up to the conferences of bishops:
1. to decide on the adaptations, within the limits laid down in the present section of the Roman Ritual;
2. to weigh carefully and prudently which elements from the traditions and culture of individual peoples may be appropriately admitted and accordingly to propose to the Apostolic See further adaptations considered to be useful or necessary that will be introduced into the liturgy with its consent;
3. to retain elements of particular rituals that may now exist, provided they are compatible with the Constitution on the Liturgy and contemporary needs, or to adapt such elements;
4. to prepare translations of the texts that are truly suited to the genius of the different languages and cultures and, whenever appropriate, to add suitable melodies for singing;
5. to adapt and enlarge this Introduction in the Roman Ritual in such a way that the ministers will fully grasp and carry out the meaning of the rites;

---

[3] See Vatican Council II, Constitution on the Liturgy *Sacrosanctum Concilium*, art. 32.

6. in editions of the liturgical books to be prepared under the direction of the conferences of bishops, to arrange the material in a format deemed to be best suited to pastoral practice; this is to be done in such a way, however, that none of the contents of this *editio typica* are omitted.

When added rubrics or texts are judged useful, these are to be set off by some typographical symbol or mark from the rubrics and texts of the Roman Ritual.

22 In drawing up particular rituals for funerals, it shall be up to the conferences of bishops:

1. to give the rite an arrangement patterned on one or more of the models, in the way indicated in no. 9;
2. to replace the formularies given in the basic rite with others taken from those in Chapter VI, should this seem advantageous;
3. to add different formularies of the same type whenever the Roman Ritual provides optional formularies (following the rule give in no. 21, 6);
4. to decide whether laypersons should be deputed to celebrate funerals (see no. 19);
5. to decree, whenever pastoral considerations dictate, omission of the sprinkling with holy water and the incensation or to substitute another rite for them;
6. to decree for funerals the liturgical color that fits in with the culture of peoples, that is not offensive to human grief, and that is an expression of Christian hope in the light of the paschal mystery.

FUNCTION OF THE PRIEST IN PREPARING AND PLANNING THE CELEBRATION

23 The priest is to make willing use of the options allowed in the rite, taking into consideration the many different situations and the wishes of the family and the community.

24 The rite provided for each model is drawn up in such a way that it can be carried out with simplicity; nevertheless the rite supplies a wide selection of texts to fit various contingencies. Thus, for example:

1. As a general rule all texts are interchangeable, in order to achieve, with the help of the community or the family, a closer reflection of the actual circumstances of each celebration.
2. Some elements are not assigned as obligatory, but are left as optional additions, as, for example, the prayer for the mourners at the home of the deceased.

3. In keeping with liturgical tradition, a wide freedom of choice is given regarding the texts provided for processions.
4. When a psalm listed or suggested for a liturgical reason may present a pastoral problem, another psalm may be substituted. Even within the psalms a verse or verses that seem to be unsuitable from a pastoral standpoint may be omitted.
5. The texts of prayers are always written in the singular, that is, for one deceased male. Accordingly, in any particular case the text is to be modified as to gender and number.
6. In prayers the lines within the parentheses may be omitted.

25   Like the entire ministry of the priest to the dead, celebration of the funeral liturgy with meaning and dignity presupposes a view of the priestly office in its inner relationship with the Christian mystery.

Among the priest's responsibilities are:
1. to be at the side of the sick and dying, as is indicated in the proper section of the Roman Ritual;
2. to impact catechesis on the meaning of Christian death;
3. to comfort the family of the deceased, to sustain them amid the anguish of their grief, to be as kind and helpful as possible, and, through the use of the resources provided and allowed in the ritual, to prepare with them a funeral celebration that has meaning for them;
4. finally, to fit the liturgy for the dead into the total setting of the liturgical life of the parish and his own pastoral ministry.

APPENDIX II

INSTRUCTION
PIAM ET CONSTANTEM
ON CREMATION

Holy Office
8 May 1963

The reverent, unbroken practice of burying the bodies of the faithful departed is something the Church has always taken pains to encourage. It has surrounded the practice with rites suited to bringing out more clearly the symbolic and religious significance of burial and has threatened with penalties those who might attack this sound practice. The Church has especially employed such sanctions in the face of hate-inspired assaults against Christian practices and traditions by those who, imbued with the animosity of their secret societies, sought to replace burial by cremation. This practice was meant to be a symbol of their antagonistic denial of Christian dogma, above all of the resurrection of the dead and the immortality of the soul.

Such an intent clearly was subjective, belonging to the mind of the proponents of cremation, not something objective, inherent in the meaning of cremation itself. Cremation does not affect the soul nor prevent God's omnipotence from restoring the body; neither, then, does it in itself include an objective denial of the dogmas mentioned.

The issue is not therefore an intrinsically evil act, opposed *per se* to the Christian religion. This has always been the thinking of the Church: in certain situations where it was or is clear that there is an upright motive for cremation, based on serious reasons, especially of public order, the Church did not and does not object to it.

There has been a change for the better in attitudes and in recent years more frequent and clearer situations impeding the practice of burial have developed. Consequently, the Holy See is receiving repeated requests for a relaxation of church discipline relative to cremation. The procedure is clearly being advocated today, not out of hatred of the Church or Christian customs, but rather for reasons for health, economics, or other reasons involving private or public order.

It is the decision of the Church to accede to the requests received, out of concern primarily for the spiritual well-being of the faithful, but also out of its awareness of other pressures. The Church therefore establishes the following.

1. All necessary measures must be taken to preserve the practice of reverently burying the faithful departed. Accordingly, through proper instruction and persuasion Ordinaries are to ensure that the faithful refrain from cremation and not discontinue the practice of burial except when forced to do so by necessity. For the Church has always maintained the practice of burial and consecrated it through liturgical rites.

2. It has seemed the wiser course, however, to relax somewhat the prescriptions of canon law touching on cremation, for two reasons. One is so that difficulties arising from contemporary circumstances may not be unduly increased; the other, so that the need for dispensation from the pertinent laws may not arise too often. Accordingly, the stipulations of CIC can. 1203, par. 2 (on carrying out a person's will to be cremated) and of can. 1240, par. 1, no. 5 (on the denial of ecclesiastical burial to a person who has left such a directive) no longer have universal binding force, but only in those cases in which it is clear that the reason for choosing cremation was either a denial of Christian dogmas, the animosity of a secret society, or hatred of the Catholic religion and the Church.

3. From this it follows that the sacraments or public prayers are not to be refused to those who have chosen cremation unless there is evidence that their choice was made on the basis of the anti-Christian motives just listed.

4. The devout attitude of the faithful toward the ecclesiastical tradition must be kept from being harmed and the Church's adverse attitude toward cremation must be clearly evident. Therefore the rites of ecclesiastical burial and the ensuing suffrages may never be carried out at the place of cremation itself, not even simply to accompany the body as it is being brought there.

The cardinals in charge of safeguarding matters of faith and morals reviewed this Instruction in a plenary meeting on 8 May 1963. Pope Paul VI at an audience granted to the Cardinal Secretary of the Holy Office on 5 July 1963 has agreed to approve it.

LETTER
COMPLURES CONFERENTIAE EPISCOPALES TO PRESIDENTS OF THE CONFERENCES OF BISHOPS ON ECCLESIASTICAL BURIAL FOR CHRISTIANS INVOLVED IN AN IRREGULAR MARRIAGE

Congregation for the Doctrine of the Faith
29 May 1973

Several conferences of bishops and many local Ordinaries have requested of this Congregation a relaxation of the discipline in force regarding the ecclesiastical burial of those faithful who at the time of their death are involved in an irregular marriage.

The Congregation carefully reviewed the opinions and recommendations that have come in on this subject and in 1972 held a plenary meeting to discuss them.

At this meeting the Fathers decided, with the approval of Pope Paul VI, that celebration of ecclesiastical burial should be made easier for those Catholics to whom it had been denied by the provisions of canon 1240.

As an amendment of this canon to the extent required, a new set of regulations will be promulgated as soon as possible. On the basis of the new arrangement the celebration of liturgical funeral rites will no longer be forbidden in the case of the faithful who, even though involved in a clearly sinful situation before their death, have maintained allegiance to the Church and have given some evidence of repentance. A necessary condition is that there be no public scandal for the rest of the faithful.

It will be possible to lessen or forestall such scandal to the faithful and the ecclesiastical community to the extent that pastors explain in an effective way the meaning of a Christian funeral. Then the majority will see the funeral as an appeal to God's mercy and as the Christian community's witness to faith in the resurrection of the dead and life eternal.

Through this letter I request that you kindly inform the Ordinaries of your conference of bishops that the text of the new decree on ecclesiastical burial will be published soon and will become effective immediately on the date of its publication.

DECREE
PATRES SACRAE CONGREGATIONIS
ON ECCLESIASTICAL BURIAL

Congregation for the Doctrine of the Faith
20 September 1973

The Fathers of the Congregation for the Doctrine of the Faith in plenary meetings on 14-15 November 1972 have decreed in regard to ecclesiastical burial: a funeral is not to be forbidden for public sinners if before death they have given some evidence of repentance and there is no danger of scandal to others of the faithful.

On 17 November 1972, at an audience granted to the undersigned Cardinal Prefect, Pope Paul VI confirmed and approved this decree and ordered its publication, thus repealing to the extent required canon 1240 par. 1; all things to the contrary notwithstanding.